T0165599

Outrageous Forgiveness
in 30 Days

The Benefits of Christlike Forgiveness

Larry Lilly
Edited By Janis Christy

WestBow
PRESS
A DIVISION OF THOMAS NELSON

WestBow Press books may be ordered through booksellers or by contacting:

WestBow Press
A Division of Thomas Nelson
1663 Liberty Drive
Bloomington, IN 47403
www.westbowpress.com
1-(866) 928-1240

Edited by Janis Christy
Photograph by Dawson Photography 426 Willow Street Terre Haute, IN 47802

ISBN: 978-1-4497-3163-2 (sc)
ISBN: 978-1-4497-3162-5 (hc)
ISBN: 978-1-4497-3161-8 (e)

Printed in the United States of America

WestBow Press rev. date: 11/18/2011

Outrageous Forgiveness in 30 Days

Also by Larry Lilly

Lasting Friendships in 30 Days
Booklets

Put in the Hole for Praying

God's Purpose in Your Pain

Golden Threads & Silver Needles

The Security of the Believer

The Rapture

The Power of 57 Cents

Christmas Reminiscence

A Tribute to Mothers

Hope for Your Darkest Night

A Christian will find it cheaper to forgive than to resent. Forgiveness saves the expense of anger, the cost of hatred, and the waste of spirits.

Hannah More

Preface

One day while praying about a painful situation, it dawned on me that I was not practicing what I had preached for years. I had to forgive the person who had seriously trespassed against me. When I did, the peace of Christ flooded my soul. I began a search for scripture passages, books, and articles on the subject and talked to people who had given or experienced outrageous forgiveness. This process literally changed my outlook on the Christian life. This book is the fruit of those years of prayerful thought.

Without Joyce, my wife of forty-seven years and the mother of our children, who is the greatest outrageous forgiver I have ever known, I could not have written this heart-moving book. This dear soul has stood by me for more than fifty years. (We were engaged several years prior to marriage and were both saved the same night fifty years ago.) She has laughed with me and a few times at me, and we have shed our share of tears, knowing that Christ will take care of the tears in His time.

Janis Christy is a longtime friend, who works in prison ministry with her husband, Don, where I met them while I was a serving a federal prison sentence. Janis also serves as executive assistant in the Office of the Vice President and General Counsel at Indiana University. She is responsible for extensive editing, thus making the book readable to English-speaking people. Thanks, Janis.

Many others have prayed with and for me in preparing *Outrageous Forgiveness* for publication. I am eternally indebted to these saints of God.

Contents

Day 1

Forgiving the Auca Indians: Normal?

I don't suppose I will ever tire of writing about forgiveness. From gossip I heard as a young believer, this must be due to the fact that I have difficulty forgiving. I can recall one Sunday, back in the age when dinosaurs roamed the earth, a dear pastor had preached that morning on the now-unmentionable sin of adultery. While eating at a deacon's house one of the dinner guests was certain that the pastor struggled with that sin, because the pastor had preached on the very same sin two years before, almost to the day. Hence, you have the theological reasoning for my conclusion that I will never cease to preach on forgiving those who trespass against me.

Sprinkled through this book, you will find an occasional story of outrageous forgiveness. The following is but one example of the powerful way lives are changed when victims practice Christlike forgiveness with no qualifying buts.

As far as I know, most Christians in the Western world have at least heard of the five missionaries killed by Auca Indians in Ecuador in 1955. Through a series of miracles of forgiveness by the widows, relatives, and friends of the martyrs, Dayuma, a young woman from the jungle, went to live with Rachel Saint, whose brother, Nate, was one of the martyred missionaries. In time, Dayuma received Christ as her Savior, and Rachel and the widows of the martyrs went into the jungle to reach the tribe for

Christ. Their success is one of the most heartwarming sagas of all time.

I was unconverted when I heard on the old radio about the slaughter of these men. Years later, I read the account in the book *Through Gates of Splendor.*

Along the line, Rachel Saint was asked, "Why did you go to those awful people who killed your brother?" Her answer brings the Southern shout to the surface, yet it also hurts my heart, as I acknowledge the hard time I have with giving forgiveness. "The fact that they killed my own brother just underscored the reason for my going to them in the first place." Quoted in Carol Hoikkala's monthly newsletter, *Hope for the Heart*, sent out primarily to female prisoners. 1.

To say the Auca Indians despitefully used the missionaries is an understatement. As I recall, over the years, the entire tribe eventually turned to Christ in faith, and several traveled the world, sharing their testimonies to that fact.

This true story has long stirred me, and after many years of pastoring and witnessing the pettiness of God's people—myself included—in obeying Jesus's commandment to forgive, I am always moved when I see or hear of amazing Christians, such as the main players in this real-life account.

Such forgiveness is not normal in the world of the lost. According to Jesus, such forgiveness should be the norm in the realm of the redeemed. Try telling this story and then make the application by asking, "Who is it that you are having trouble forgiving, and just what has that person done to you?" An awkward silence usually falls on the meeting like a pile driver. May the Lord Jesus help us!

The forgiveness freely given by the surviving missionaries to the Auca Indians is counter to prevailing notions of forgiveness given by the offended person. Most writing on the subject grant

Christian forgiveness with one hand and then take it away with the other by demanding some redeeming work on the part of the offender.

Although I recognize several levels of forgiveness, the highest level—the level emphasized in this book and the one that I do not fully grasp—is the level mentioned by Paul in Romans 5:8. "But God commendeth his love toward us, in that, while we were yet sinners, Christ died for us."

The surviving missionaries and certain family members of those martyred forgave the Auca Indians long before the poor savages thought about asking for it. Isn't that the kind of forgiveness Paul describes?

Keep in mind that the purpose of this book is to encourage the *giving* of forgiveness rather than *receiving* it.

Day 2

Grandson Forgives Grandmother's Killer

On Tuesday, March 24, 2009, I heard Bill Pelke speak. To say that Bill is unusual is putting it mildly. Bill has put the biblical doctrine of forgiving others into glaring practice, so much in the manner of Jesus that he shames most of us who claim to teach the truth of forgiveness in Jesus.

Bill's grandmother, Ruth Pelke, whom he fondly called Nana, was a noted children's Bible teacher and a well-rounded Christian who loved Jesus and her church. On May 14, 1985, Ruth answered her door to three ninth-grade girls, who asked her to teach a Bible lesson to them. Once inside the house, one girl hit Ruth on the head with a vase. Two of the teens ransacked the house, while Paula Cooper used a twelve-inch butcher knife to stab Nana thirty-three times. The girls found $10, took the keys to Ruth's old car, picked up a friend and drove around for a while. Ruth's son found her mutilated body the next day. Altogether four teenaged girls had been involved in some way in the murder/robbery.

According to the judge in the case, Paula Cooper was the dominant personality, and, ultimately, Paula was sentenced to die in Indiana's electric chair. Bill thought this was the appropriate sentence.

One night while working his shift as an overhead crane operator at Bethlehem Steel, Bill fell into deep thought about his grandmother. He saw a photograph of her with tears of Christ's love and compassion streaming down her face. God moved in a powerful way, and Bill accepted the power to forgive Paula Cooper. Miraculously, God used Bill and others to bring about a reprieve for Paula, reducing her sentence to sixty years. I wept as Bill told his story. With tears in his eyes, Bill said, "Had she been executed, I would have walked hand-in-hand with her to the chamber."

Bill emphasized the truth taught by Jesus: "Revenge is *never* the answer."

Bill was not and is *not* a bleeding-heart liberal but was raised in a fundamentalist church (General Association of Regular Baptists) and graduated from the bare-knuckled Hyles Anderson College.

As Bill held audiences spellbound in two venues, I thought how miserably I have failed to teach and demonstrate the forgiveness Christ taught and demonstrated.

Much of the bickering I am called on to umpire results from refusal to forgive the pettiest things imaginable. Yet, this man demonstrates the near-ultimate forgiveness, the ultimate being given by Christ during His passion when He prayed, "Father forgive them, for they know not what they do." Luke 23:34

During her imprisonment, Paula Cooper has earned a GED, a college degree, and has made a profession of faith in Jesus Christ. She is scheduled for early release in 2014. Is her profession real? Time will tell, but one thing is for sure—her forgiveness from Bill is the real thing.

This story is certainly outrageous. The truth is that most of us will never be confronted with the opportunity to exercise or receive this degree of outrageous forgiveness. This is a very good thing. But the Lord has commanded us to forgive freely those who have trespassed against us. As I understand His words, obeying Him is not optional, and I cannot have inner peace until I do as He says in this most important matter.

In Matthew 18:34, Jesus tells of the torment that we will endure if we refuse to forgive. I will comment at length on this verse later, but for now, hide the words of verse 35 in your heart: "So likewise shall my heavenly Father do also unto you, if ye from your hearts forgive not every one his brother their trespasses."

Like the stormy sea that Jesus calmed, much of the internal turmoil in our lives can be calmed by obeying the command to forgive. I use extreme examples in this book in the hope that you will see the importance of personally forgiving those who have wronged you in much lesser ways.

Day 3

You Just Forgave Them?

Today's lesson is one that I have learned to call a "billy-goat truth." As many read this and realize the implications, I know I will receive notes of protestation that begin, but I want to say at the outset that God is not a billy goat, and His grace has no buts. Pause and ponder the greatness of the forgiveness God demonstrated at Calvary.

A confessed friend of mine, Mel Branham, sent me the following piece. It's the story of Peter and Linda Biehl. I had never heard of them either. I'm using Mel's information, since I couldn't find the story in any of my other sources, and it needs telling. It seems to me that evangelical newspapers should have shouted this from the rooftops. Or should they? The fathomless depth of biblical forgiveness eludes most religious people. First, let's read Linda's statement and then consider how she and Peter go beyond mere forgiveness.

"Everyone says, 'You just forgave them?'"

"My husband and I talked about this a lot. Yes, forgiveness is one part of it, but the real challenge—and what I think South Africa is about—is the reconciliation aspect. And reconciliation is about work. You can forgive someone and walk away and go on with your life, but if you're going to make a real difference and work at changing conditions, it's more about the reconciliation process, the coming together and going forward mutually. It's taking things that are negative and turning them into positive energy."

You now know that the story has origins in Africa. Here's more.

Linda was referring to Ntobeko Peni and Easy Nofemela. These two men were part of a group that murdered Amy Biehl, Peter and Linda's daughter, while she helped to register voters in an election. The Biehls are white. The other two men are black and have been forgiven by the two white parents.

But wait! That's not all. Peni and Nofemela asked, "Why do they forgive us?"

Any sensible person understands that these two men do not deserve forgiveness. And that's the point. No one deserves God's forgiveness either, but it's freely available in Christ. And there's more.

In addition to forgiving the two men, the Biehls started a foundation to promote healing with a logo of one white hand and one black hand intertwined and the slogan,

Weaving a Barrier Against Violence

Need I tell you that Mr. Peni and Mr. Nofemela work for this organization as paid employees?

I certainly hope Christians discover this kind of forgiveness. It could revolutionize the world.

I checked to see if Jesus ever talked about this, and sure enough, He did. Luke 23:34: "Then said Jesus, 'Father, forgive them; for they know not what they do.' And they parted his raiment, and cast lots."

While many do not grasp the significance of this statement, claiming that only the Roman soldiers were included in this prayer, it seems quite apparent to me that Christ included a broader group, as Paul clearly demonstrates in 1 Corinthians 2:8: "Which none of the *princes of this world knew:* for had they known it, they would not have crucified the Lord of glory" (emphasis mine).

Noted Bible commentator and pastor of First Presbyterian Church of Philadelphia for thirty-seven years, gallantly anti-slavery Dr. Albert Barns states, "Ignorance does not excuse altogether a crime if the ignorance be willful, but it diminishes its guilt. They had evidence; they might have learned his [Jesus'] character; they might have known what they were doing, and they might be held answerable for all this. But Jesus here shows the compassion of his heart, and as they were really ignorant, whatever might have been the cause of their ignorance, he implores God to pardon them. He even urges it as a reason why they should be pardoned, that they were ignorant of what they were doing; and though men are often guilty for their ignorance, yet God often in compassion overlooks it, averts his anger, and grants them the blessings of pardon and life."

There exists a plethora of arguments against this kind of forgiveness, though close inspection reveals an unwillingness to forgive. The forgiveness of Christ does not release one from the responsibility to forgive as He commanded.

Outrageous forgiveness can only flow forth from a heart warmed by close proximity to Jesus.

Jesus not only talked about outrageous forgiveness, He demonstrated it graphically.

Day 4

Remarkably Outrageous Forgiveness

"They are truly remarkable people." Edward Rollins, attorney.

Counselor Rollins was speaking at the sentencing of his client, Emily Wessel, twenty-four, of Bethesda, Maryland.

Ms. Wessel had admitted that she was driving while impaired (heroin), resulting in a crash that killed fifty-five-year-old truck driver Vincent Urie.

Dorothy Urie, Vincent's widow, read a four-page letter to the judge, part of which said, "Your honor, I can truly say that I have no hatred or animosity toward Emily. I forgive her and believe that Jesus loves her and wants to change her life. I would welcome the opportunity to share with her."

I have observed several courtroom trials, many of them involving Christians, including one of my own, and I have never witnessed anything like the State vs. Wessel proceeding. Usually it is quite the opposite.

Mrs. Urie continued her plea for leniency for Emily by stating, "Vincent was an avid golfer, who was often nicknamed Preach for his penchant for talking about Jesus."

She also recounted that just before he died, her husband was talking to a friend about Jesus and how much He loved her.

Attorney Rollins stated, "In twenty-three years of practicing law, I've never had anything like this. It's incredible."

'Tis a sad commentary, indeed, that an experienced attorney in a town (Elkton, Maryland), which is home to numerous faithful churches, has never witnessed such forgiveness.

In my forty-nine years as a preacher/pastor, I have heard every reason on earth, heaven, and other remote places as vain attempts to justify an attitude of vengeance, the refusal to forgive. One man said, "Due to the enormity, we can't let this go."

The statement was made relative to a financial matter. Many professing Christians assume money is of greater enormity than the life of a truck driver, husband, and father.

Most honest pastors know that within the walls of their sanctuary dwell some unmentionables, names that if mentioned in a positive, forgiving way would ignite a war that would do Al-Qaida proud.

Keep in mind that the newspaper from which this story comes is a secular, county paper, *The Cecil Whig*. I am acquainted with the grandfather and father of Counselor Rollins, but I do not know Edward.

Why is it that one of the quintessential planks of the Christian faith is so very seldom demonstrated? Could it be, perish the thought, that most apparent Christianity is mere Sunday-go-to-meeting window dressing?

Mrs. Dorothy Urie holds a place of Christian nobility in the eyes and hearts of those of us who struggle with actually practicing biblical forgiveness of the highest level.

God's grace is utterly out of this world.

Day 5

Outrageous Incarceration

I received a nice letter from my friend Pastor Jim Grove, in which he enclosed a list of quotes covering numerous subjects. One in particular caught my eye. Quotes, verses, and experiences based on this theme always catch my eye, for the subject is one of the most misunderstood in all of Christianity.

No, I'm not talking about the mystery of the Trinity, though wars have been fought over that one. More wars have and are being fought over forgiveness, the one I will rant and rave on today. Failure to understand and act on this one is the cause of many wars—national, marital, and personal. "To forgive is to set the prisoner free and then discover the prisoner was you," says Pastor Jim Grove.

I rejoice in the forgiveness I experience through the merits of Jesus Christ. I don't think I could live without knowing of His all-encompassing forgiveness. God has forgiven me for Christ's sake, not because I deserve it or because my sincerity is flawless, but for Christ's sake.

Today's quote states that when I forgive, I set the prisoner free, and that means I am free from the bitterness that invades my heart on refusal to forgive.

This means that the person who has offended me in word or deed, the one who has caused me pain or loss, will go unpunished by me. To forgive in the biblical sense means that I forgo my right to vengeance, my right to exact punishment, for that which is forgiven is evermore considered unusable as evidence. Most understand this to the point of self-application. But it also applies to those who trespass against me. When I truly forgive from the heart, the person who sinned against me may never be called on to pay up personally. How can this be? When I forgave, didn't I turn it over to God, for His wise punishment?

Certainly.

If God for Christ's sake has forgiven you, and thus your sin is paid for in full by the blood Jesus shed on Calvary, it follows that those who sin against you may also have all their sins, including the ones perpetrated against you, paid for by Christ.

I Corinthians 13 plainly teaches that God's love and the love we are supposed to reflect does not keep an account of wrongs done. The only way to follow this mandate is to develop the habit of forgiving. The math Jesus taught in Matthew 18:22, "Jesus saith unto him, I say not unto thee, Until seven times: but, Until seventy times seven," is the ground for forming this simple practice of habitually forgiving wrongs: $70 \times 7 = 490$ times. We learn by repetition, and it takes a lot of repeating to get into the very good, Christian habit of forgiving.

It is well established that until we forgive, the person from whom we withhold forgiveness is in fact our personal, tyrannical corrections officer, always there to prod and infuriate us at the very thought or mention of his or her name. In the most absolute sense, the person you refuse to forgive is your captor. He or she determines your level of heart peace, your level of mental well-being, and if left unattended long enough, your physical health.

A pastor told me of a dirty trick that had been played on him, which had caused great pain and loss, even causing some members to leave the church. Although enraged, he stated, "Justice demands satisfaction, and I will not rest until I see justice smiling."

This dear man spent many years in actual torment until he was set free. It happened late one night, as he was studying for a sermon on the finished work of Christ. When he forgave, he was set free and according to his testimony, enjoyed a sound sleep for the first time in years.

You could put Pastor Grove's quote into practice and have a great experience beginning today:

"To forgive is to set the prisoner free and then discover the prisoner was you."

Day 6

Let Go Revenge? Outrageous.

A short while ago, I wrote a piece on abandoning the desire for revenge on those who have trespassed against us. Predictably, the ol' mailbox was filled with responses. Victims want their pound of flesh. Humanly speaking, rightly so. Why did Paul say in Romas 12:19 "'Vengeance is mine, I will repay'"? He knew Jesus understands our human condition and how much we suffer at the hands of others. He does not want us to contribute to that suffering by internal thoughts and emotions that multiply the damage. The concept of *Lex Talionis*, the Old Testament rule of eye for eye, the demand for retaliation in kind tends to have a boomerang effect and puts the claws of the law deeper into the person who insists on the eagle's vengeance than into the flesh of the offender.

It troubles me deeply when adherents of non-Christian religions demonstrate a more Christlike attitude about getting even with others than do Christians, who know the Bible and are professed followers of the Galilean.

I discovered a key in a speech by a non-Christian leader, the Dalai Lama.

> The Dalai Lama shows no anger toward the Chinese even though the policy of the Chinese government for years has been to practice genocide toward Tibetans; culturicide

toward their institutions, beliefs and everything they hold dear; and geocide toward the very land they live on. When asked about his apparent lack of anger toward the Chinese and he replied, "They have taken everything from us; should I let them take my mind as well?" 1.

How is it that the Dalai Lama, a man who is proclaimed to be the current manifestation of God on earth, understands a Christian principle that even Christian clergy fail to grasp?

Jesus Christ taught that the desire for vengeance is such a potent elixir that mere humans cannot withstand what it does to them. The desire to get even seldom, if ever, results in the person upon whom we desire to see the brimstone of God's wrath poured out getting their just due. Much to my own dismay, I have watched helplessly as some who have mistreated me have gone to Jesus and received forgiveness. He never even consulted me about it. He just forgave them. The nerve.

In a mad demand for revenge, many are destroying themselves. How many nights of sleep are lost fretting over God's apparent lack of judgment against those who trespass against us? How much heart peace is lost to thoughts of torment for others, because rather than forgive, we insist on playing God and getting even our way? We refuse to take into account that being an offended human, a victim, does not give us the knowledge of the future or the ability to see how the Lord is working on His big picture.

Many crazy things are done in a futile search for revenge. Is this what the Dalai Lama meant when he said, "They have taken everything from us; should I let them take my mind as well?" 2.

We cannot undo the things that people have done to us. Certainly, the Dalai Lama is helpless to make China pay. Nor can you truly make those who have misused you pay.

So, what to do?

Give it to Jesus.

That's right. When I forgive, I give up all future claims against the person forgiven. When I do this, I trust God to right any wrong in whatever manner He sees fit. He often deals with those who trespass against me at the cross. If you understand what happened at the cross, this is the most severe punishment imaginable.

If someone has taken something from you, the only sensible thing to give in return is forgiveness, not your peace of mind and heart.

Matthew 6:14 says, "For if ye forgive men their trespasses, your heavenly Father will also forgive you."

The gospel's forgiveness passages broadly teach that our failure to forgive others on the same basis that we are forgiven is evidence that we do not have an adequate grasp of the forgiveness given to us on the merits of Christ's sacrifice.

Orlando Aloysius Battista, author of seventeen books, the first being, *God's World and You*, wrote, "One of the most lasting pleasures you can experience is the feeling that comes over you when you genuinely forgive an enemy; whether he knows about it or not." 3.

Day 7

Justice Satisfied Outrageously

In the course of life, you will meet all kinds of people. In this voyage, many people will do despicable things to you. Their words and actions will hurt every fiber of your being.

How do you deal with this reality? Do you ignore it? Do you distance yourself from it by denying that it happens? How? By keeping the old, "Chin up, Son," approach?

There are about as many ways to forgive as there are people. The trouble is that there is only one that really works.

Emperor Marcus Aurelius formed the habit of starting each day with the following statement to himself about himself: "Today you will meet all kinds of unpleasant people; they will hurt you, and injure you, and insult you; but you cannot live like that; you know better, for you are a man in whom the Spirit of God dwells." 1.

This man refused to operate at a level he correctly deemed to be beneath his human dignity. Many allude to him as a super nice guy. Knowing that he gave the order to martyr Christians removes any luster he may have otherwise had in my mind.

Marcus believed he was God, walking around on the earth. Many people and governments still harbor this mistaken idea very close their heart. Yet, you have to admit that the philosophy of Marcus Aurelius is better than many that are predicated strictly on vengeance. Marcus refused to sink to the level of fire with fire, tit for tat, and so should those who know Christ in a personal way. Marcus thought the Spirit of God dwelt in him.

We who know Christ are assured that God's Holy Spirit does, in fact, dwell in us and empowers us to live above the methods of the world around us. How sad to see so many act as though God were dead, at least in practical matters.

As Christians, we might do well to rephrase the emperor's comment thusly:

> Today you will meet all kinds of unpleasant people; they will hurt you, and injure you, and insult you; but you cannot live like that; you know better, for you are a *Christian* in whom the *Holy* Spirit of God dwells.

I changed one word and added one word to the statement. If applied, it will change your life from one of bitterness, pettiness, and a vengeful attitude into one of peace, acceptance, and forgiveness.

I was recently approached to consider writing a booklet on the matter of learning to forgive. Part of the deal was that it had to be secular. I pondered this for all of thirty seconds. In any secular system of forgiveness, any true reason to forgive is absent. The strongest reason in the secular world to forgive is that doing so is good for you. The problem is that this does not deal with the offense. You may invent any number of forgiveness mechanisms, none of which will be sufficient to satisfy the yearning for justice.

To understand the need for justice to be satisfied, you must visit Calvary and see what God thinks of sin. You must grasp the fact that the words and actions of your life are so horrible that they placed God's Son on the cross, and that God can and does forgive you on the basis of Christ's suffering alone. Only then can you understand Christ's statement, "'Father, forgive them; for they know not what they do.'" Luke 23:34

Those who trespass against you have access to the same forgiveness in Christ that you have.

So, why are you harboring a grudge? With what part of Christ's sacrifice are you not satisfied? What greater price can be paid?

Day 8

Winds of Forgiveness

Two friends were walking through the desert. At some point in the journey, they had an argument, and one slapped the other in the face. The man who was slapped said nothing but knelt and wrote in the sand,

Today my best friend slapped me in the face.

They kept walking and came upon an oasis, where they decided to bathe in the cool water. The one who had been slapped became stuck in some mire and was drowning, but his friend saved him. After recovering, he carved on a stone:

Today my best friend saved my life.

The friend asked, "After I hurt you, you wrote in the sand, and now you carve on a stone. Why?"

The friend replied, "When someone hurts us, we should write it down in sand, where the winds of forgiveness can erase it away. But when someone does something good for us, we must engrave it in stone, where no wind can ever erase it."

Learn to write your hurts in the sand and to carve your blessings in stone.

I talked with a man who, years ago, was accused of some terrible things. In the course of time, the church he attended wrote him, stating that he was forgiven by the church. He showed the letter to me and said, "Larry, the thing that really hurts is that to this day, people from that church will rehash the events with all the gory details. I thought when something is forgiven, it's no longer mentioned, even in heaven, that holiest of all places."

I called the said church and asked about this brother. He was right; I got my ear full. God knows nothing of this type of forgiveness, for that is not what true forgiveness does. One of my favorite old time songs, "The Old Account Was Settled Long Ago," has a phrase that says, "And the record's clear today, for He washed my sins away, when the old account was settled long ago."

One of the many definitions of forgiveness that I identify with and use often when I'm preaching is from Ephesians 4:32: "And be ye kind one to another, tenderhearted, forgiving one another, even as God for Christ's sake hath forgiven you." As I understand this scripture, the sins forgiven by God for Jesus' sake are rendered unusable as evidence, because they are under the blood. This means that if I have forgiven you on the same basis that God forgave you—for Christ's sake—I cannot go into the stack of evidence marked "Inadmissible" and use it as an exhibit against you.

How often the Court of the Bitter Heart goes against the High Court of Heaven and permits blood-stained evidence to enter the record. You can be certain that such will be reversed on appeal to Christ.

The good that is done to or for us in Christ's name is always welcome in the presence of the Lord. Remember the good times, the good words spoken, and the good deeds done. You will feel better and live longer. And the Lord will permit you to talk about the good others have done for you. He really would rather that you remain silent about all of your good deeds and let the record speak for itself.

Learn to write your hurts in the sand and to carve your blessings in stone.

The late, great, German actress Marlene Dietrich, wrote:

> Once a woman forgives her man, she must not reheat his sins for breakfast.

Day 9

To Kiss the Robe of God

The purpose of this book is to give ICU treatment to the cause of learning and practicing biblical forgiveness. For the most part, I do not deal with other aspects of forgiveness, though they are important. I find they often put the cart before the horse to the neglect of the proper order as set forth in the scripture.

In his book about forgiveness, reconciliation, reparation, and revenge, *Bone to Pick*, author Ellis Cose makes a grand statement: "To forgive the truly horrible is to kiss the robe of God, to emulate no less a figure than the dying Jesus Christ." 1.

We used to call such eloquence an oratorical flight to realms celestial.

As I said earlier in this book, I write about forgiveness, because I have so much difficulty practicing it. I tend to find myself submerged in the quagmire of bitterness, or at least hoping those who trespass against me get theirs—and the sooner the better!

In his book *Forgiveness Is a Choice*, author Robert Enright states:

> Forgiveness means responding to unjust hurt with compassion, with benevolence, perhaps even with love. While it does not deny the right to resentment, it does not wallow in bitterness; nor does it necessarily demand that the perpetrator respond with gratitude or grace. 2.

I am comforted in the knowledge that I am not alone in my reluctance to forgive. I am also comforted knowing that there is a growing body of literature that takes the biblical position on the importance of freely forgiving, as Christ did.

Life will see to it that each of us receives our share of pain. The preponderance of scriptural evidence supports the fact that God is using these events to give us opportunities to grow in Christ or to wallow in self-pity.

Job is a case in point.

This ancient man of means and character suffered personal loss when his sons and daughters were killed. He suffered pecuniary loss beyond measure, and he suffered physical loss when the Lord permitted Satan to take his health. Job had enough sense to realize that all of this was above him, so rather than engage in second-guessing God, he simply trusted Him all the more.

Here's the application for our personal use.

Failure to forgive is actually failure to trust God to work things out. It is failure to believe the well-worn verse in Romans that assures us that all things really do work together for good if we love the Lord. Romans 8:28: "And we know that all things work together for good to them that love God, to them who are the called according to his purpose."

God is on record concerning His saints, that vengeance is His, that He will repay, that we are to practice forgiveness in the manner laid out in the Bible, simply, "that we forgive one another as God for Christ sake has forgiven us." Ephesians 4:32. Recently our church sign proclaimed to all who passed:

To forgive means I give up the right to hurt back.

We must dig down deep in our hearts and ask the Lord to push us on to a higher level of spirituality, to the level where we will find a reason to forgive, rather than state all the reasons to continue in hate and its accompanying misery. May we enter into the depth of the words of Jesus in Luke 23:34, "'Father, forgive them …'"

> When a deep injury is done to us, we never recover until we forgive. (Alan Paton)

Day 10

Twenty Years from Now

About twenty-five years ago, I read a book that intrigued me. I have often thought about it in the passing years. It was lost in a fire at our home, April 20, 1997.

The main character in the book was a traveling man, and one day he checked into a room. When he walked into the room, a man was sitting in a chair. The man in the chair assured our character that he was in the right room. He began to talk about how things had been over the past twenty years. As he wrapped up his story, he told our main character that he, the stranger, was the man our character would be in twenty years.

Have you ever wondered what it would be like to know what you will be like in twenty years? Most of us at least entertain the thought from time to time, and it needn't frighten you. For the most part, who you will be twenty years from now, barring death or catastrophic illness, is reasonably predictable.

Twenty years from now, you will be defined by what you think about the most.

As a rule, people pour into their life the energy required to become who they think they want to be or to do what they want to do.

This is good and also very dangerous.

I knew a man thirty-five years ago who was consumed with getting even with another man, who had done him wrong. After the lapse of twenty years, he was a sour, old man. His every thought was dominated by the memory of the wrong committed against him. There is no doubt that he was done wrong. Tragically, he committed a greater wrong against himself. He became so bitter and so eaten away inside that he ended his life by his own hand. Several of his friends, including me, tried to help him, but to no avail.

I often joke that I first heard the concept of becoming what we think about the most when I was a teenager. I was in danger of becoming a tall, brunette teacher. After my conversion to Christ, I began to see the importance of the teachings of Christ about sowing and reaping, of letting things go that are destructive by their very nature.

An attitude of revenge is self-destructive. It's tragic that our modern churches do not, as a rule, teach the full truth concerning biblical forgiveness as demonstrated by Jesus Christ. Forgiveness may or may not do the person you're forgiving any good; they may scoff at the idea.

And many do.

The purpose of true forgiveness is what moderns would call therapeutic for the person giving the forgiveness, more so than for the person needing forgiveness.

Think about it. When the Bible says that God has forgiven you for Christ's sake, this means that God has agreed on the basis of Christ's sacrifice to forgo vengeance for your sin against Him. Christ paid for your wrong. When you refuse to forgive, you are doing something that God does not sanction in your life: engaging in the lust for revenge. Revenge belongs to Him.

Lex Talionis refers to the law of the talon, the image of an eagle stabbing its claws into prey and carrying it off. Too many of the

Lord's people wish to stab into the heart and life of any who offend or hurt them. To forgive means to give up the legal, or Lex, right to hurt the person who hurt you in the same or greater way. Forgiving a person is to refuse to place your talons (claws) into his or her heart.

An old story posits an eagle swooping down and catching a huge fish just above Niagara Falls. The fish was too heavy for the eagle, but the eagle would not release the fish from its talons. The eagle, still clutching the fish, died in the raging rapids just below the falls. When you thrust your as it were talons into a person and refuse to forgive, you will eventually pay a terrible price. Eagles have a natural right to fish. Humans want revenge, but we also have the supernatural right in Christ to release the person who has offended through forgiveness and rise above the hurt with a special joy in their heart.

Twenty years from now, who you are will be determined to a larger degree than you think by your willingness or refusal to practice forgiveness as demonstrated by Jesus Christ.

Consider these words from Paul in Colossians 3:13: "Forbearing one another, and forgiving one another, if any man have a quarrel against any: even as Christ forgave you, so also do ye."

Day 11

Five Key Words

Many years ago, while in the "gated community" (euphemism for federal prison), I read a helpful article regarding the importance of forgetting behaviors that have been forgiven. We've all heard and probably used the phrase, "Well, I forgive, but I just can't forget."

The apostle Paul gives some great help in Philippians 3:13–14:

> Brethren, I count not myself to have apprehended: but this one thing I do, forgetting those things which are behind, and reaching forth unto those things which are before, I press toward the mark for the prize of the high calling of God in Christ Jesus.

These two verses are loaded with keys to overcoming the torment of the inability to forget.

The lexicon gives one definition of forgetting as no longer caring for. Through faith in Christ, we can and should reach a point of no longer caring about the things of the past.

The following five words help to keep this in perspective.

Reject

Anger is keeping a meticulous record of who did what to you or hatred toward those who have misused you.

Replace

Hatred with love, anger with kindness.

Refuse

To continue to ruminate about the many wrongs, the slights, and the covert and overt villainous acts against you or loved ones. The context of our text is really the high achievements of Paul, and he is teaching that we must not attempt to live in past glory or pain. Refuse to retaliate, even if you get the chance.

Refocus

From past failure to future dreams of success. Looking back hinders any attempt to make progress. I remember a line from a song of my childhood about, "A star up there that's beckoning, along the heavenly way." Emerson encouraged motivated people to, "Hitch your wagon to a star." 1.

In the above verse Paul is pointing to the bright and morning star and giving us the proper direction for life. The story is told of a man who was losing his memory. In order to treat this problem, he risked losing his eyesight. He thought about it for a while and then said something like, "I will keep my vision, for I would rather see where I'm going, than remember where I've been!"

Rely

On the Lord. I find some peace in knowing the Lord has forgiven me for things that despite all my efforts could never be made right in this life. I have to rely on the power of Christ's sacrifice to pay for my sins. In line with this truth, I must accept that many of the things others have done to hurt me have been forgiven by the Lord on the basis of Christ's sacrifice. If it works for me, it has to work for them.

The Lord can and will give us the power to no longer care for the things that hinder us by holding dear the memory of wrongs done and the venomous dreams of vengeance.

In Romans 12:9, the Apostle makes it clear that God knows the end from the beginning and will right all wrongs: "Dearly beloved, avenge not yourselves, but rather give place unto wrath: for it is written, 'Vengeance is mine; I will repay,' saith the Lord."

Talking with many people who have come through very tough circumstances, I find that some seem to nurse the traumatic events of yesterday, or in the case of a downfall, will not accept the fact that today God is real and His care and promises concerning the future are more certain than the sunrise.

We can be slaves to memories of the past or soldiers, marching toward God's promises.

Day 12

Larry Lilly Is not Jesus. So?

For many years, I have enjoyed preaching and teaching that men and women must learn to forgive those who do mean things to them. The Bible is clear on this. Over the course of those years, I have witnessed many people overcome bitterness, anger, have their blood pressure lowered, and experience any number of other very good things that come about as a result of sincerely forgiving those who have wronged them.

I have no difficulty at all preaching this dynamic biblical truth to my listeners.

I personally have no trouble forgiving those who have trespassed against you. This enabling grace helps to keep me from being overwhelmed with anger and bitterness. I have forgiven those who trespass against others so often that it's almost a conditioned reflex on my part. God has brought about this deep spiritual maturity in my life.

Where I struggle is in overcoming anger, bitterness, and myriad other tormenting attitudes I tend to harbor against those who trespass against me. You would think that because it's so easy for me to forgive those who trespass against you, it would be as easy to forgive those who despitefully use me.

Such is not the case.

I'm aware that Jesus forgave those men who mocked Him, who spit on Him, beat Him, and ultimately nailed Him to the cross. He forgave them.

I find comfort in nursing thoughts of vengeance against those who wrong me by recognizing that Larry Lilly is not Jesus. So, a little carnal retribution might be a good thing to teach those turkeys who sin against my person or my name.

Such thoughts as the above help me to maintain a high level of righteous indignation at the base manner in which I have been treated. You should forgive your enemies, but my enemies are of a different stripe. Therefore, God expects me to hate them.

I actually heard a man say, "I know I should forgive, but does the principle of forgiveness apply to something of this magnitude?" I assume it hadn't dawned on his pea brain that Calvary was the most outrageous event in history from a human perspective.

In checking the scriptures concerning forgiveness, it's plain that I am to forgive those who do me wrong. This is a bitter pill, but it's the truth.

I must accept that I need the Spirit of Jesus to practice true forgiveness. I must ask Him to make me willing to forgive and to place those actions and words against me in the pile of forgiven evidence stamped with the seal of Christ's blood, so they cannot be recalled as evidence against the offending person or persons.

This is so easy to preach to others!

To do?

Surely, you jest.

Luke 11:4 says, "And forgive us our sins; for we also forgive every one that is indebted to us. And lead us not into temptation; but deliver us from evil."

C. S. Lewis wrote, "Everyone says forgiveness is a lovely idea, until they have something to forgive." 1.

I know the truth of this statement. How are you doing in forgiving?

Day 13

Rebellion, Rejection, and Restoration

A dear friend of many years wrote in response to an article on forgiveness:

> I heard a statement the other day: "I can forgive him, but I can't accept him." I suppose the statement could mean, "I have forgiven, but I don't condone his sin." However, it was along the lines of, "He has hurt so many, and he has a lot to do to make it right." What would you think?

I am using a Bible event to respond, though those who are not fully aware of the grace bestowed on them in Christ will refuse to see the scope of God's forgiveness by attempting to justify the mean-spirited, writing off of people rather than embrace the restorative power of Christ.

A grand battle between two great men took place. The verses below tell about the event, the recommendation, and the personal use of one at one time considered unfit:

> Acts 15:37–39: "And Barnabas determined to take with them John, whose surname was Mark. But Paul thought it not good to take him with them, who departed from them from Pamphylia, and went not with them to the work. And the contention was so sharp between them,

that they departed asunder one from the other: and so Barnabas took Mark, and sailed unto Cyprus."

Colossians 4:10: "Aristarchus, my fellow prisoner saluteth you, and Marcus, sister's son to Barnabas, (touching whom ye received commandments: if he come unto you, receive him;)"

2 Timothy 4:1: "Only Luke is with me. Take Mark, and bring him with thee: for he is profitable to me for the ministry."

Paul saw a serious flaw in Mark, and the ensuing argument is recorded.

Somewhere along the line, Mark overcame the flaw through Christ's power and the mentoring of Barnabas. Fourteen years later, Paul recommends Mark to the church at Colossae and then requests the presence of Mark with him at Rome, as he sees Mark as profitable to the ministry.

Over the years, Mark had demonstrated that he understood the seriousness of his offense and served the Lord passionately. So, Paul extended to Mark that which he had himself received: grace.

The idea of forgiving and restoring if the offender pays some humongous price is foreign to grace. We all owe a debt we can never repay, and we who have received grace must bestow this grace upon others. Paul, Mark, and Onesimus, in the book of Philemon, are a case study of this principle.

As to worrying about condoning forgiven sin, the statement on its face bears evidence the person has *not* forgiven, for when sin is forgiven, there is nothing to condone.

When sin is forgiven, it is erased from the books of heaven, and numerous verses used by biblical writers attest to this awesome fact. Here are a few:

> Micah 7:19 "He will turn again, he will have compassion upon us; he will subdue our iniquities; and thou wilt cast all their sins into the depths of the sea."

> Luke 1:77 "To give knowledge of salvation unto his people by the remission of their sins."

> Hebrews 8:12 "For I will be merciful to their unrighteousness, and their sins and their iniquities will I remember no more."

According to scripture, the sin is gone, or "under the blood," as the old-timers and the Bible state, and can no longer be presented as evidence.

Today, I will rejoice in the forgiven men and women God has used along the way to help and encourage me to continue faithfully serving Jesus.

Day 14

Forgiveness: Attribute of the Strong

I have been working on this book about forgiveness for several years and have found that this elusive, essential act is often missing in the modern abnormal Christian, abnormal meaning a knowing willful departure from the normal, as forgiving is the norm for God's children, who are walking with Jesus in the Christian life. I am still learning the art of forgiving. It's tougher than you might think.

According to R. T. Kendall, in his book *Total Forgiveness*, former president Jimmy Carter, Archbishop Desmond Tutu, and Elisabeth Elliot promoted a $10 million Campaign for Forgiveness Research, designed to attract donations to fund research proposals. The John Templeton Foundation awarded research grants to twenty-nine scholars, and one of the primary discoveries of these studies is that: The person who gains the most from forgiveness is the person who does the forgiving. —R. T. Kendal

I have preached this biblical truth for more than forty-nine years. I should have been contacted by the Foundation. The Great Blonde asserts that having to put up with me (the Grouchy Bear) abundantly qualifies her as an ascended master on forgiveness. Well, we missed another boatload of cash.

One Sunday morning, I preached to the gathered saints a gem titled

"Ignorance: The Cause of Unforgiveness."

The failure to forgive reveals ignorance of several truths.

The evidences of failure to forgive are spiritual agony, guilt, emotional trauma, and physical pain. Can you imagine the threefold suffering of Joseph's brothers due to their unwillingness to forgive him and their father for the teen antics of Joseph? Genesis 50:15 shows the boomerang effect of the failure to forgive: "And when Joseph's brethren saw that their father was dead, they said, Joseph will peradventure hate us, and will certainly requite us all the evil which we did unto him."

They had failed to practice forgiveness, therefore, they feared they would be treated in the same way.

Refusal to forgive is to ignore reason. When you write off someone, you cut yourself off from the benefit of the gift the Lord has given to this person.

Many individuals and groups are shipwrecked due to the refusal to accept the gift from someone they refuse to forgive. The unforgiven person goes about his or her life, bringing blessings to anyone who will receive them and their gift from the Lord.

To harbor an unforgiving spirit is to ignore the biblical teaching on the subject. About ninety verses deal with forgiving others. At the very least, Jesus taught that our peace of mind is dependent on forgiving those who trespass against us.

Finally, to refuse to forgive is to deny the example of Jesus at Calvary. As He was being crucified, He prayed, "'Father, forgive them.'"Luke 23:34.

I seriously doubt if the list of unforgivable things that we maintain comes close to the enormity of Calvary.

I am often amazed at the insight of some folks who do not accept Christ concerning the meaty things of faith. Consider the following:

> The weak can never forgive. Forgiveness is the attribute of the strong. —Mahatma Mohandas Gandhi

So, is your forgiver working?

Romans 4:7: "Saying, Blessed are they whose iniquities are forgiven, and whose sins are covered."

Day 15

Replaying Dirty Tricks

Have you ever wondered why it's so important to learn the art of forgiving others?

There are a number of reasons, most of which I have shared over the years when preaching on forgiveness. Yet, I still learn more as I ask for wisdom in this area. The essence of forgiving someone is, by the grace of God, to let them off the hook, by the grace of God, as God has done for me. The word "forgive" in the Greek means to send along, to release.

The scripture insists that when God forgives, He also forgets. This does not mean that God has selective Alzheimer's, but He has rendered the forgiven offense to be inadmissible in any further proceedings. It's easy to say this, but to actually do it, is another story.

God sets the example of forgiving and forgetting in order for us to maintain a healthy mind and heart.

Ken Crockett wrote in the *911 Handbook*, "Every time we recall an injury, we hit the replay button on the VCR of our minds and we get wounded one more time." 1.

In my experience, the recurring wounds can be more severe than the original. Here's why.

When the original offense takes place, we find some comfort in telling ourselves that this act won't stand, that surely God will ride in with heavenly cavalry and right this wrong. Often He does not. Who knows why? I don't.

So, the offense goes unchallenged and unpunished, and I suffer from an unrequited desire for vengeance. Time does not heal this wound. Time and memory bring about a festering sore in my heart, mind, and soul. Each time I hit the replay button, the agony of soul gets a little worse, my heart cries out, and the event is recorded ever deeper into my heart. Janis Christy commented on this truth when she wrote, "Just an aside, science has proven (as we already know from scripture) that replaying these things burns bad circuitry into our brain as well. Our brains, of course are connected to our bodies that seem all too often to respond with absolute cooperation to the bad things our brains tell them." 2.

The replaying of the event often leads to addenda that include a time of getting even. I see in my mind and feel in my heart the joy and exhilaration of this wrong being made right, of this turkey getting what's coming to him—with a little more added for the pain and suffering caused to me and my loved ones.

With each playing, the saga of my victimhood becomes more dramatic.

And then.

And then reality comes back on the scene, and I must again cope with the fact that the unforgiven perpetrator of the deed at least seems to be escaping any form of judgment—from God or man—and I must tread the globe, knowing that someone committed an offense against me, and he or she will continue to live unpunished. With my luck, the person will experience some kind of grace from God, and because Christ paid for the sin, will never be called into account for it. It's just not fair. I am a victim, and as such, my thoughts should rank higher than the idea of God forgiving anyone without my consent.

For your own sake, be careful with the replay button on the VCR activating the video of dirty tricks played on me.

A more effective and healing practice is to get back to the Bible and reread the scenes from the stories that deal with great forgiveness granted to undeserving people who had committed enormous sins, even to the point of atrocity, against the hero of the story.

Joseph is a case study. His brothers were scared to death that he would kill them, which he had the authority to do, as he spoke with words of fire and forgiveness in Genesis 50:20: "But as for you, ye thought evil against me; but God meant it unto good, to bring to pass, as it is this day, to save much people alive."

We must learn to accept the truth of Romans 8:28: "And we know that all things work together for good to them that love God, to them who are the called according to his purpose."

We quote this verse often, and we should act accordingly. Joseph learned that the mean-spirited actions of his brothers, who wanted him dead, while they meant evil, were used by God to bring growth in Joseph and preserve Israel.

The Lord has an overriding purpose for good, even when people perpetrate evil against you.

Day 16

Forgiveness: A Touch of the Divine

When I mentioned I was putting this book together, Mom (now gone on) said, "The book on forgiveness." I am several years behind schedule, self-imposed, but I keep learning more about the why and kind of forgiveness I am supposed to extend.

Just this week, as I was rethinking the account of the Prodigal Son, his father, and the contrast in philosophy concerning forgiving, I was again moved by our human refusal to accept the higher level of forgiveness. The story, as told by Jesus, is found in Luke 15:11–24:

> And he said, A certain man had two sons: And the younger of them said to his father, Father, give me the portion of goods that falleth to me. And he divided unto them his living. And not many days after the younger son gathered all together, and took his journey into a far country, and there wasted his substance with riotous living. And when he had spent all, there arose a mighty famine in that land; and he began to be in want. And he went and joined himself to a citizen of that country; and he sent him into his fields to feed swine. And he would fain have filled his belly with the husks that the swine did eat: and no man gave unto him. And when he came to himself, he said, How many hired servants of my father's have bread enough and to spare, and I perish with hunger!

> I will arise and go to my father, and will say unto him, Father, I have sinned against heaven, and before thee, And am no more worthy to be called thy son: make me as one of thy hired servants. And he arose, and came to his father. But when he was yet a great way off, his father saw him, and had compassion, and ran, and fell on his neck, and kissed him. And the son said unto him, Father, I have sinned against heaven, and in thy sight, and am no more worthy to be called thy son. But the father said to his servants, Bring forth the best robe, and put it on him; and put a ring on his hand, and shoes on his feet: And bring hither the fatted calf, and kill it; and let us eat, and be merry: For this my son was dead, and is alive again; he was lost, and is found. And they began to be merry.

In his desire for forgiveness from his father, the Prodigal posited in his mind, while still in the hog pen, just what he would say to his dad, how he would say it, and the grounds on which he would ask for forgiveness. His reasoning is the reasoning of most of humanity—saved or lost—and the kind of forgiveness he asked for is the only kind most people are willing to extend, whether or not they profess faith.

Look at his reasoning and petition to the father: "'I have sinned against heaven, and before thee, and am no more worthy to be called thy son: make me as one of thy hired servants.'"

He recognized his wrong action against God and against his father. He also recognized that sin devalues relationships in the normal course of things; therefore, he is willing to relinquish his claim to Sonship and is willing to be a mere servant, a hired or field servant.

The kind of repentance he demonstrated is acted out each day all around us; perhaps by us. The kind of forgiveness he asked for is requested every day and is given every day. It's a high level of human forgiveness in that life itself is not forfeited.

I have spent my entire adult life as a Christian who is appalled at the total lack of understanding of the scope of God's forgiveness, as opposed to the kind we ask for and receive. Surely, you know that if you receive forgiveness from a vast majority of people, not only including but especially Christian people, it will be the kind asked for by the Prodigal. It's human, and I suppose it's better than no forgiveness, but not by much.

God's forgiveness is vastly different.

In the midst of the son's pouring forth his petition, the father interrupts and utters conditions of forgiveness that put our version to shame, as well it should. He sees his son, falls on his neck in a tender, welcome embrace, and has compassion on him. He commands the best robe to be placed on the son, along with the emblems of leadership and great family responsibility. Rather than a time of morbid trial to see if this is real, it's a time of affirmation, designation, and promotion. The truth of promotion just dawned on me for this writing. The Prodigal was willing to cease claiming Sonship and be treated as a lowly servant. The father received him, not as a servant, but as a son and promoted him to the position of family representative, much to the chagrin of the elder brother.

In life, we often place limits on what God will do for us, and we do this with no scriptural basis. God does a wonderful thing when He takes away all our sins. He does the same for those who trespass against us. We are always in line, either with Satan and make no provision to forgive, or we are human and dish out petty ideas that reflect that they are human at best. Or we emulate God, who freely forgives all of our sins on the basis of the sacrifice of Christ.

A painting in the Louvre depicts a boy, striding angrily along a lane away from a peasant's farmhouse. Standing in the doorway of the humble home, a father is leaning out, face flushed in rage, waving a fist, as if to say, "And don't come back." Just inside the house, the artist shows a mother, wringing her hands in an apron, tears scalding her cheeks.

Another painting, hanging alongside the previously mentioned one, shows the now much older son trudging back up the lane toward the house. The idea of making amends saturates the scene. The door to the house is open, and just inside, we see the mother, wringing her hands in her apron. The father is lying in state in a coffin of roughhewn lumber, death having sealed off forever the hope of forgiveness to both father and son.

The time for forgiveness of the divine order is now, before it's too late.

So, how are you doing? Are you into no forgiveness, human forgiveness, or do you extend a touch of the divine?

Day 17

Forgiving Parental Sins

"You're a very lovely daughter."

Senator Strom Thurmond to Essie May Williams. 1.

So?

Essie May, now seventy-eight, is a retired teacher and the daughter of the good Senator and Carrie Butler. Senator Thurmond was twenty-two and Carrie was sixteen when they had an affair. Essie is the fruit, or in those days, the issue of their passion.

So?

Carrie was a sixteen-year-old maid, working in the Thurmond home.

So?

Carrie was black.

So?

How times have changed.

The affair took place in 1925. I assure you, "So?" was not the response of that long ago day.

In most of the southern states, various laws were passed, making it illegal for members of different races to marry; these were known as miscegenation laws. Typically a felony, miscegenation laws prohibited the solemnization of weddings between races and prohibited the officiating of such ceremonies. Sometimes, the individuals attempting to marry would not be held guilty of miscegenation themselves, but felony charges of adultery or fornication would more usually be leveled against them. Most such laws have been repealed in the United States and, where still on the books, have not been enforced, having been struck down in 1967 by the US Supreme Court in Loving v. Virginia.

And this in the land of Pocahontas? Pocahontas a young Indian girl married Captain John Smith at Jamestown and moved with him to London, England where as a Christian, (Converted heathen) she was a celebrity and a truly outstanding Christian woman.

It's a long day from 1925 to 1967 and much water under the bridge.

I have no way of knowing whether, under different circumstances, Mr. Thurmond would have made an honest woman of Carrie. Seeing as how he claimed belief in Christ, I would hope so. Many people who practiced miscegenation (mixing of the races) moved to other states to avoid prosecution. Others, well, you probably read the story or saw it on TV.

In light of the times of Strom Thurmond and Carrie Butler, I suppose Strom did what he could. And I am deeply moved by the understanding of Essie May.

This lovely daughter must have spent more than one lonely night longing for the perks of the rest of family. And yet, she is satisfied with the simple acknowledgment by the senator and now the entire family. Such is life.

Of course, there is a spiritual and practical application to this story.

You don't have to live like a victim because of someone else's sin. Essie enjoyed great peace and success.

And you don't have to hide under the house because you have engaged in a sinful, stupid act. You receive God's forgiveness in Christ and go on. When God forgives you, you can even become a US senator.

Essie demonstrated her gigantic greatness as a Christian in that she forgave Mr. Thurmond.

I wish I could find words powerful enough to get it through some pretty thick skulls to quit fighting with life. No matter what sins your parents committed upon you, no one gains anything if you continue to attempt to live while eaten up with bitterness. Christ swallowed the bitter pill of Calvary with joy to purchase your forgiveness and to provide a reason for forgiving others.

Malachi 4:6: "And he shall turn the heart of the fathers to the children, and the heart of the children to their fathers, lest I come and smite the earth with a curse."

Day 18

A Connecticut Yankee on Forgiveness

My calling as a preacher of the gospel entails some interesting meetings, conversations, and attempts at explaining the finer points of aspects that many take for granted—all while engaging in only partial application of the doctrine/principle at hand.

Forgiving, being forgiven, and forgiveness rest somewhere near the top of the list.

As I talked with a man I have known for years, he brought up some trouble that he had in the past, in which he was deeply hurt by fellow Christians. In passing, he remarked, "Larry, it is much easier to forgive enemies than it is to forgive friends or family."

My friend spoke the truth. Yet, the Bible addresses this tough action and thereby wipes away all excuses for continuing to harbor thoughts of vengeance against our friends or family who have willfully brought hurt into our relationship.

I asked my friend, "Have you truly forgiven?"

With a scowl on his face, a steely glint in his eye, and a suddenly clinched fist he replied, "Of course."

He then noticed how tightly his fist was clinched, and said, "Well, pretty much."

The truth of the matter is that while he has not taken physical vengeance, he has not forgiven in the biblical sense. He is still bitter just under the surface.

A grand commentator on the passing scene of an earlier time, Mark Twain, commented on true forgiveness with this: "Forgiveness is the fragrance the violet sheds on the heel that has crushed it." 1.

Jesus Christ practiced this kind of forgiveness.

The rest of us preach it.

The above-mentioned "Connecticut Yankee in the Theologian's Court" knew what real forgiveness looks like, which may account for his well-publicized low opinion of those of us who proclaim we are followers of Christ, the "Great Forgiver."

Commenting on the great forgiveness we owe to our friends and loved ones who sin against us, Paul put it thusly in Romans 5:8–10:

> But God commendeth his love toward us, in that, while we were yet sinners, Christ died for us. *Much more* then, being now justified by his blood, we shall be saved from wrath through him. For if, when we were enemies, we were reconciled to God by the death of his Son, *much more,* being reconciled, we shall be saved by his life.

The italics of "much more" are mine to emphasize the fact that, as does God, so must we in the matter of forgiving fully those who have hurt us the most.

Mr. Twain's comment is needed now far more than when he wrote it. Again, I am amazed at the way many skeptics grasp what we who profess faith are supposed to do, while we wander all around the fencepost, searching for a valid reason to disobey the plain command and example of Christ concerning forgiving from the heart.

"Forgiveness is the fragrance the violet sheds on the heel that has crushed it." —Mark Twain

Day 19

Peace or Torment

In a study of the concept and practice of forgiving, it is nearly impossible to fail to notice several levels of forgiveness on the part of the forgiver. Tragically, most Christians never rise above a basic level and, therefore, never enter the joy of the highest level, the exemplary level demonstrated, for instance, by Jesus Christ and of all people, including Esau.

You are aware that the initial action of Christian forgiveness is to be carried out by the offended, the victim, not because of any merit of the offender, but on the basis of Christ having paid for the sins of others against us through His sacrifice on Calvary.

Paul clearly lays the outline of forgiving when he states in Ephesians 4:32: "And be ye kind one to another, tenderhearted, forgiving one another, even as God for Christ's sake hath forgiven you."

Luke records the utterance of Christ on the cross in Luke 23:34: "Then said Jesus, Father, forgive them; for they know not what they do." Luke 23:24.

That this prayer of Jesus is to be followed is driven home with sledgehammer intensity by Stephen's words, uttered as he died by stoning, as Paul stood close by, holding cloaks of his executioners:

And they stoned Stephen, calling upon God, and saying, Lord Jesus, receive my spirit. And he kneeled down, and cried with a loud voice, Lord, lay not this sin to their charge. And when he had said this, he fell asleep. (Acts 7:59–60)

It is common for victims to say, "Oh, yes, but that was Jesus, and He is God in flesh. And Stephen was one of the first deacons and a preacher. I can't be expected to forgive on that level." How much do you want to bet? Paul already gave the answer in Ephesians 4:32: "And be ye kind one to another, tenderhearted, forgiving one another, *even as God for Christ's sake hath forgiven you*" (emphasis mine).

So much for appealing to Jesus and the saints. Let's look at a man who is tragic in life and a very bitter man, yet one who gave the kind of forgiveness we are studying.

We know from the Old and New Testaments that Esau lived and died a reprobate concerning the faith. He was a bitter womanizer and never repented, though he often wept bitter tears over his chosen lifestyle. Yet, he did something that shames modern Christians.

What did Jacob do to give Esau any reason to forgive him for taking advantage of his weakness? The only thing I can find that Jacob ever did concerning his cheating Esau was to live in fear of the consequences of his actions.

Yet, in the meeting between Esau and Jacob some thirty years after the offense, the initial sin of taking deceitful advantage, Esau comes out as the paragon of giving forgiveness. Why do we who claim such holiness permit a bitter, sexually impure man to outdo us in one of the most Christlike actions possible for a human to emulate? When you set someone free through Christ's forgiveness, the one set free is, in reality, you.

A friend of many years, Dr. George Monday, sent the following to me, and it touched on the inner agony of Jacob and of all who engage in activities that take advantage of friends or brothers. George commented:

> Jesus told a story about forgiveness after he had taught the disciples about prayer and forgiveness, Matthew 18. After the fellow who had received such forgiveness refused to return the same kindness to his fellow, he was reported to the lord who had freely forgiven him. His lord ordered that he be turned over to the tormentors. I saw something that gave me understanding this in I John 4:18: "There is no fear in love; but perfect love casteth out fear: because fear hath torment. He that feareth is not made perfect in love."
>
> Now there is our word, torment. The tormentors are all the negative emotions caused by disobedience: fear, anxiety, guilt, worry, etc. Those who refuse to exercise free and unlimited forgiveness are placing themselves in an emotional prison that is going to be excruciating and cause a lot of restless nights of tossing and turning.

I have a special place in my heart for this brother, who took a stand as my friend in the dark night of my life. He is on the money with the insight he shared in the above paragraphs.

Some time ago, I talked with a man who said that he has trouble each time a particular man comes to mind. Each time this man enters his life through seeing him, or seeing something or someone who reminds my friend of this man, he relives a hurtful experience and will lie awake for nights, fuming over what should have been done to the man, even to the point of enjoying wringing the man's neck personally!

I know this brother well enough to believe that if he were actually to wring the man's neck, he would do it as unto the Lord! The man whom the mere mention of his name evokes such wrath has moved on with his life and goes about as though he has good sense.

Perhaps he does. He has peace; my friend has bitterness, though in the initial sinful act, he was in the right.

Which man is better off? The man who has peace does not in any way trick the other man out of his peace. The bitter man has made the choice for bitterness and torment over the peace that passes all understanding.

Not a good choice.

Do you enjoy the peace of God, or do you live in torment? The choice really is yours.

Consider again the last words of the martyr, Stephen:

> And they stoned Stephen, calling upon God, and saying, Lord Jesus, receive my spirit. And he kneeled down, and cried with a loud voice, Lord, lay not this sin to their charge. And when he had said this, he fell asleep. (Acts 7:59–60)

If Stephen could pray for his murderers, surely you and I can pray for those who give us dirty looks, can't we?

Day 20

Amish Forgiveness: Outrageous

If you have Jesus in your heart and He has forgiven you,
how can you not forgive other people?

—Rhita Rhoads

Most Christians around the world were moved to the depths of
human grief by the brutal murder of five Amish girls, ranging in
age from seven to thirteen, while they were in their one-room
schoolhouse in Lancaster County, Pennsylvania, on October 2,
2006. I wept when I heard and read about it. (Google "Amish
murder" for details.)

Nickel Mines is about twenty miles from my hometown, and I
have driven through the area many times. In those days, I usually
had a few religious out-of-context names for the horse and buggies
that held me up as I tried to drive like a maniac (Joyce's words).

One headline proclaimed that the Amish community was taking
up money for the family of Charles Carl Roberts, the murderer
of the children. The article stated that the community was going
to great lengths to let his survivors know they wanted the wife
and children to continue living in the community and that they
had no hard feelings toward them. And furthermore, they had
forgiven Charles Roberts. Mr. Roberts was mad at God over the
death of his daughter right after birth nine years before. He also

mentioned he had molested two female relatives when he was twelve, twenty years ago.

The names of the children who were murdered and their ages:

Naomi Rose Ebersol	age 7
Marian Stoltzfus Fisher	age 13
Anna Mae Stoltzfus	age 12
Lena Zook Miller	age 7
Mary Liz Miller	age 8

What a price was paid for a long-held grudge against God and the repressed guilt of childhood crimes.

In response to the Christian love demonstrated to Marie Roberts, the widow of Charles, she wrote this to the Amish community:

> Your love for our family has helped to provide the healing we so desperately need. Gifts you've given have touched our hearts in a way no words can describe. Your compassion has reached beyond our family, beyond our community, and is changing our world, and for this we sincerely thank you.

It struck me that the fundamental difference between the Old Order Amish and my style of Baptist is not the 1850s clothing or the quaint customs, such as driving a horse and buggy and using no electricity or other modern conveniences, but something far deeper than outward appearance.

The difference is expressed in an ABC News piece by Charles Gibson. Midwife Rhita Rhoads, who was present for the birth of two of the five murdered children, said "If you have Jesus in your heart and He has forgiven you, how can you not forgive other people?" 1.

Again I quote Rhita Rhoads, "If you have Jesus in your heart and He has forgiven you, how can you not forgive other people?"

Anybody want to take on the question?

Don't feel bad, because you have company: namely, the bulk of professing Christendom. Yet, consider the comments of those who are not Amish but who have studied them over the years. Many criticized the Amish for their near instant, total forgiveness of the murderer. They had all of the arguments you hear each day, ad infinitum: forgiveness is inappropriate when no remorse has been expressed; you're running the risk of denying evil, and so on.

Donald Kraybill, noted scholar of Amish life, stated:

> Letting go of grudges is a deeply rooted value in Amish culture, which remembers forgiving martyrs, Dirk Willems who gave his life trying to save an enemy who was attempting to kill him and Jesus himself. The Amish willingness to forgo vengeance does not undo the tragedy or pardon the wrong, but rather constitutes a first step toward a future that is more hopeful. 2.

I assure you that over long years, I have heard every reason on earth for refusing to forgive those who trespass against us.

I, for one, believe that a revival of true forgiveness in our Christian groups would spark a revival of faith such as the world has never seen. All Christians give lip service to the command of Jesus to forgive. When we begin to practice this forgiveness from the heart, the world will stop for at least a few minutes in wide-eyed wonder, proclaiming:

We have never seen it like this before.

The murders were committed on October 2, 2006. On October 12, 2006, the tiny school was torn down, the ground where it stood was plowed under, and grass was sown. The reason for this is to reinforce the Amish teaching:

That which is forgiven has never been. (Unknown)

Though this deep, Christian truth is, for the most part, forgotten by the church membership at large, it is clearly taught in scriptures such as Hebrews 8:12: "For I will be merciful to their unrighteousness, and their sins and their iniquities will I remember no more."

Psalm 103:12: "As far as the east is from the west, so far hath he removed our transgressions from us."

This biblical teaching helps the believers to cease dwelling on the pain and to focus on forgiveness. As Paul Boese states, "Forgiveness does not change the past, but it does enlarge the future." 3.

When rebuked by e-mailers for doing a story on the Amish murders, news commentator Greta Van Susteren wrote these moving words, "On the other hand, I want people to know about the Amish. I am in awe of them—especially their ability to practice what they preach. They actually do forgive—many people talk about forgiveness, but can't or don't do it."

So, how are you doing in the area of forgiving those who have trespassed against you? Most of the slights committed against us are trivial in comparison to the Lancaster County slaughter. Could it be that these people have a better grip on the teaching of Jesus than we religious sophisticates?

Oh, yes, one more thing. The families of the wounded and the murdered children attended the funeral of Charles Carl Roberts and took up an offering for his family.

If you have Jesus in your heart and He has forgiven you, how can you not forgive other people?

—Rhita Rhoads

Day 21

A Convict's Contribution

You will never know how many thousands of times I thought and rethought these ideas while hurting in that box. —David Marshall (Carbine) Williams 1.

The above is from a man who spent endless days in solitary confinement. Rather than using the time to feel sorry for himself, he thought about a subject that would propel him to fame and save countless thousands of lives.

Today's hero began making what was called the best moonshine whiskey in the mountains of North Carolina at the tender age of nineteen. At age twenty-one, during a raid on his still, a deputy sheriff was killed. Our man pleaded guilty to second-degree murder and was sentenced to twenty to thirty years in the penitentiary.

At the request of the sheriff and the widow of the slain deputy, his sentence was commuted after ten years.

Being a country boy, he initially had trouble adjusting to prison. As a result, he spent countless days in solitary, the hole, the box. Unlike thousands of others who have had a similar experience, he demonstrated the reality that men (and women) are redeemable.

He also demonstrated Paul's truth that when bad things happen as a result of your actions, you can overcome and go on to victory by improving the quality of your attitude and work.

Most of us will not have the opportunity of a major contribution resulting in thousands of lives being spared, as did David Marshall Williams. But we do have the obligation to quit worrying about what we can't change and go to work on becoming reliable people who are committed to excellence of performance.

Keep in mind that it was the forgiveness given to David by the widow of the slain deputy sheriff that contributed greatly to his recovery, and this outrageous forgiveness contributed to victory in the Pacific Theater during World War II.

The ideas that David nurtured while hurting in the box were put into practice while he worked in the prison machine shop. The mechanism he put together from scrap iron and an old fencepost was said by General MacArthur to be, "one of the strongest contributing factors to our victory in the Pacific." 2. His contribution was so great and his life such a demonstration of victory over adversity that a movie was made of his life. The film starred Jimmy Stewart, who was very much like the character he portrayed in the film *Carbine Williams*.

Mr. Williams was not proud of the action that sent him to prison. Sane people who do dumb things are never proud of such actions. But you must accept God's way of dealing with such events and get on with life. Carbine Williams did this, and many a GI knew he owed the inventor of the M1 Carbine something by the end of WWII.

I tell stories like this in the hope that I can rekindle the belief in the hearts of Christians and Americans that we must stop throwing away people. And I write in the hope of helping men and women who have done the dumb thing to demonstrate the power of Christ by being willing to improve the quality of their life and their work and to do the thing they do with all their might as unto the Lord.

> You will never know how many thousands of times I thought and rethought these ideas while hurting in that box. —Carbine Williams 1.

While you're hurting in the box of your current experience, think on the things Christ has done for you. You never know what wonder may come from this.

Saul, the forgiven man who was changed to Paul, commented on his response to God's forgiveness to him in harmony with Stephen's dying prayer. Stephen, as he breathed his last breath while being stoned to death at the instigation of Paul, said, "Lord, lay not this sin to their charge." Paul stated in 1 Corinthians 15:9–10:

> For I am the least of the apostles, that am not meet to be called an apostle, because I persecuted the church of God. But by the grace of God I am what I am: and his grace which was bestowed upon me was not in vain; but I laboured more abundantly than they all: yet not I, but the grace of God which was with me.

Paul accepted the grace of God and of Stephen and unreservedly threw himself into the work the Lord had given to him, as he expresses in his phrase, "Labored more abundantly than they all."

Day 22

A Martyr's Manly Request

"How could I have been so terribly afraid? I must ask you both to forgive me my weakness. Today I know for certain that I should have done otherwise."

Have you ever been afraid and, as result of that fear, done or failed to do something and later felt deep remorse and shame? I admit to having been afraid and later ashamed on too many occasions in my life.

Fear is the common enemy of the human race. Many of the inner problems we face are rooted in fear. Worry is a symptom of fear.

Preachers tell people that to worry is a sin, because it suggests that God may not be in control of a given situation. Then, the preacher lies awake and worries that his sermon may have offended someone.

"How could I have been so terribly afraid? I must ask you both to forgive me my weakness. Today I know for certain that I should have done otherwise."

A famous Christian wrote this amazing statement of repentance to his sister and her husband several months after refusing to help them in a time of grief. He had followed the advice of a church superintendent.

At the time, the repentant man was torn in many areas of his life. His entire world was set ablaze, and he was ripped apart by the political storm with Adolf Hitler at the center. The incident was the request by his sister to perform the funeral ceremony for her father-in-law.

His sister had married a Jew, who converted to Christ. In spite of the conversion, the family did not meet the requirements concerning marriage of the Aryan law introduced by Hitler, hence the potential for serious conflict with the government and his church.

"How could I have been so terribly afraid? I must ask both of you to forgive me my weakness. Today I know for certain that I should have done otherwise."

Factoring in that this brother was a little bit afraid of Hitler and the Nazi juggernaut rolling across Germany, and soon the world, we can find forgiveness for Dietrich Bonhoeffer. I tell of this episode in this martyr's life to remind you that none of us are always fearless; none of us always do the right thing.

All of us humans are subject to fits of fear.

I have admired Pastor Bonhoeffer for many years. Not that I'm sure I could stand up to Hitler (the Great Blond—my wife— strikes fear in my heart with but a look). I identify with him because I know what it's like to be afraid. The fear of failure, of rejection, of ejection, and many other fears have robbed me of many a blessing.

In the situation here, Bonhoeffer faced not only Hitler but the sting of ostracism from his church. The *frown of the brethren* has brought many an otherwise brave soul into submission.

Over the long haul Bonhoeffer found the courage to stand true, to overcome his fears.

While his brethren, for the most part, wanted to suck their thumbs and pray for better days, Bonhoeffer found the courage of Christ to do what he could. That's really all any of us can do. That's all the Lord expects.

Because our Lord Jesus understands, we can say with Bonhoeffer, "Today, I know for certain that I should have done otherwise."

And then we go on.

Today, can you think of anyone who has caved in to some fear? Do you hold the person in contempt? Do you grasp the truth that it is better to understand and forgive?

Honestly, I have more trouble asking for forgiveness than I do giving it. Doing both is essential in developing the spiritual life. The apostle Peter wrote in 2 Peter 3:18, "But grow in grace, and in the knowledge of our Lord and Saviour Jesus Christ. To him be glory both now and forever. Amen."

Day 23

A Racetrack Man on Forgiveness

"You don't throw a whole life away just because it's banged up a little."

In order to be near Mother, I was born in Havre de Grace, Maryland, a little burg located where, "the Susquehanna River pours itself into the Northern tip of the Chesapeake Bay," as James Michener stated in his grand *Chesapeake.*

This part of my early life was brought to mind when I read the obituary of Seabiscuit, penned by Red Smith in the May 20, 1947, *New York Herald Tribune.* He mentioned the racetracks where the noted horse held records. I recall seeing the track in Havre de Grace as a kid and having my grandmother tell me that Seabiscuit had raced there. My grandmother was deeply religious and was able to take her darling grandson to tour the racetrack only because the almost divine Seabiscuit had, "appeared there," as my grandmother put it. She said to me,

"Larry, horses are smarter than people, because horses never bet on people."

As a man, I never bet on horses, but as a pastor, I bet on people all the time. That's what redemption is about: betting that through Christ, people can rise above their faults and their failures to run with persistence the race the Lord has laid out for them.

This chapter was birthed when I heard a supercilious religious critic trash the book *Seabiscuit,* by Laura Hillenbrand, due to the language and less-than-Puritan life of the characters.

I read Laura's masterpiece and, recalling racetrack people from my early days, I assure you Laura's characters are understated and seem almost churchy compared to the real thing. As a matter of fact (here come the piles of remonstrance and outrage, but I will stand here), I found more about redemption/forgiveness in that story than in most Baptist churches, to which expression of faith I confess to adhere.

When you manage to boil away the setting, Laura's book is not about Seabiscuit or racing*: it's about struggling all the way up from all the way down, be ye man or beast!*

In the book, Laura has Tom Smith, the eventual trainer of Seabiscuit, rescue a horse that is about to be shot because it has an injured hoof. Tom later tells Charles Howard, the eventual owner of Seabiscuit, why he rescued and nursed the horse. His statement became the guiding philosophy of the team:

"You don't throw a whole life away just because it's banged up a little."

Tom continues by pointing out what the horse can be rather than what it cannot be.

I listened (I eavesdrop all the time) as two men discussed their church's search for a new pastor. They are of another persuasion, so it felt great to listen and privately critique their comments. They were discussing their failure to find any unbesmirched candidate for the office. I admit that a few they mentioned were certainly smirched, but I chuckled as I thought,

I wonder which of the besmirched men may be their congregation's Seabiscuit.

You never know. Nor will they!

Jesus instructs His audience in Luke 7:47, "'Wherefore I say unto thee, her sins, which are many, are forgiven; for she loved much: but to whom little is forgiven, the same loveth little.'"

Sometimes, a man or woman is injured in the hoof, and thus, his or her walk is hindered. Yet, tender love and forgiveness can help someone on the journey, and loving much, the individual can go on to profitable service, as did the fugitive slave mention by Paul in the book of Philemon.

Learning to forgive and then doing it sets you free to receive a greater blessing, often from the one to whom you have extended forgiveness.

"You don't throw a whole life away just because it's banged up a little."

Day 24

Forgiveness Imprinted on the Heart

The Great Blond is preparing a book review for a future issue of my monthly newsletter, *Larry Lilly's Journal.* The book under Joyce's eagle eye is by Francine Rivers: *The Last Sin Eater.*

The story is set in the Smoky Mountains circa 1850 and is a saga of faith-breaking superstition. The catalyst is a ten-year-old girl who leads the tiny community to faith in Christ, as she points out the heresy of the Sin Eater and the truth of Christ.

The basic mountain legend usually portrays the Sin Eater as a deranged man who would place food on a person's body, living or dead, and after performing a ritual, would expiate the person's sin by eating the food. To perform this ceremony, the Sin Eater usually required a small fee. After all, it must be worth something to have your sin taken away.

This practice seems strange to modern people, yet I actually met a man who claimed to have the power of a Sin Eater. He lived in a remote place in the mountains of southwest Virginia. He was the last of the breed, I hope, and was loony to the max.

The idea of a person having the gift or power to eat the sins of another is a perversion of the truth that Christ took away our sins in His sacrifice on Calvary. An often overlooked fact in the sacrificial death of Christ for us is that, "He who knew no sin became *sin* for us" (2 Corinthians 5:21; emphasis added).

The truth is that while on the cross of Calvary, Christ became the embodiment of sin, and the wrath of a righteous God was loosed on Him. He suffered the eternal punishment for our sin. This is Christianity 101, yet current literature seems to ignore this biblical truth. The principle is laid out plainly in 2 Corinthians 5:17–21:

> Therefore if any man be in Christ, he is a new creature: old things are passed away; behold, all things are become new. And all things are of God, who hath reconciled us to himself by Jesus Christ, and hath given to us the ministry of reconciliation; To wit, that God was in Christ, reconciling the world unto himself, not imputing their trespasses unto them; and hath committed unto us the word of reconciliation. Now then we are ambassadors for Christ, as though God did beseech you by us: we pray you in Christ's stead, be ye reconciled to God. For he hath made him to be sin for us, who knew no sin; that we might be made the righteousness of God in him.

The reality that Christ took away our sin was made clear to me years ago, when my pastor helped me to grasp the reality of the substitutionary death of Christ. In simple words, Christ died for me. He died in my place. And mystery of mysteries, according to Galatians 2:20, "I am crucified with Christ: nevertheless I live; yet not I, but Christ liveth in me: and the life which I now live in the flesh I live by the faith of the Son of God, who loved me, and gave himself for me." I was somehow in Christ when he died. Through faith, I am identified with Him as having died as the penalty demanded by the law. I am also identified with Christ in His resurrection and walk in newness of life. Romans 6:1–14 makes this wonderful truth as plain as can be.

I am going to great lengths to keep this chapter from being overly "preachy." I know I am failing in this noble aspiration, but please take the time to study the scripture and to recognize the truth of the gospel when you see or hear it.

The deep, inner need for forgiveness is carved into the human heart. And man has formulated thousands of ways to escape from or at least placate the guilt associated with sin. None of these inventions actually work, by the way.

To know that our sins are taken away, we must join the paean of praise in Revelation 1:5:6: "And from Jesus Christ, who is the faithful witness, and the first begotten of the dead, and the prince of the kings of the earth. Unto him that loved us, and washed us from our sins in his own blood, And hath made us kings and priests unto God and his Father; to him be glory and dominion for ever and ever. Amen."

I am a sinner saved by grace, and I, therefore, remain mystified by the grace of God. I rejoice in my spirit at the truth of a gospel song that has tragically fallen into disuse in many fellowships. The first verse says, "What can wash away my sin, nothing but the blood of Jesus."

The song then follows the entire course of the Soterion (the entire scope of salvation).

When we come to a biblical inner knowledge and appreciation of the enormity of our own sin and the incomparable price paid by Jesus Christ for our forgiveness, we then are to give the same kind of forgiveness to others—undeserving others, mind you—that He has freely given to us.

The biblical words for forgiving all mean essentially the same thing. The Hebrew *kaphar* means "to cover." *Nasa* means "to lift away," and *salach* "to send away." The primary Greek word is *apouluo*, and the two other are simply variations, depending on the context. "Forgive" in the New Testament expands a little on the Old, meaning, "to free fully, relieve, release, dismiss, depart, let die, pardon, let go, send away, set at liberty."

In Hebrew, Greek, English, or any tongue you may choose, we are provided no excuse for refusing to forgive those who trespass against us. I am especially fond of the definitive "let die." That which is dead is to be buried, hopefully somewhere other than in my heart or mind.

In forgiving others, it is imperative to bury that which is forgiven. The Old Testament portrays the truth of a Christian song illustrated in the story of the Scapegoat. After an animal was slain, the priest laid hands on the goat, representing the sins of the people, thus putting the sins of the people on the Scapegoat. The goat was released into the wilderness, representing the sins being sent away or removed from them. Later, the goat was found, and there was no evidence of the sin. This ritual is found in Leviticus 16. The shadow meaning is expressed in these lyrics:

> Living he loved me, dying he saved me, buried he carried my sins far way, rising he justified freely forever, one day he's coming, O' glorious day.

When we freely forgive someone from the heart, we must learn the biblical truth of the above and put it into practice.

As Christ sent away our sin, we are to send away the sin of those who sin against us.

Day 25

Forgiving for a Safer Tomorrow

"We cannot undo yesterday. We must use today for a safer tomorrow." 1.

Back in 2005, when I wrote the piece on the Sin Eater, I received a large number of notes about the piece. In spite of that, I wrote again on the futile practices around the world to expiate sin. "Expiate" is a $50 word that means to get rid of.

Articles over the last decade addressing the genocidal practices in Uganda and surrounding countries have told stories of unimaginable suffering. Many young children were kidnapped from their home villages and forced to become soldiers for the marauding bands of cutthroats masquerading as liberation forces. Some of these children were six or seven years old. They were given machine guns and told to kill. And many did so with the gusto of a beer commercial. They killed fellow villagers, ripped unborn children from the wombs of mothers, and slaughtered the infants.

How is that for kindergarten hands-on experience?

Many of these young butchers are now making their way home and desire to be restored to family and to the group at large. Can this ever work? How?

When the young butchers confess to the surviving villagers the surviving, offended villagers take the confession of guilt and the desire for forgiveness at face value and are willing to start from this point. One village chief said, "We cannot undo yesterday. We must use today for a safer tomorrow." 2.

This concept sounds good to me.

I attempt to help people who have committed serious offenses against others, and I also often try to help those who have suffered offense—in other words, victims.

It's much more difficult to help victims, for so many make a career of being a victim. Many on both sides of this offender/victim scenario demonstrate their lack of understanding. In response to that lack, a village chieftain in the heart of an African jungle has responded with more common sense and inner peace than we religious sophisticates in America. And we carry a Bible.

One ritual that shows repentance on the part of the offender is a simple one that involves an egg. That's right, an egg.

The man or woman who wants to come home and enjoy acceptance by peers stands at the outer boundary of the village, breaks an egg, and with sandals removed, dips a toe into the egg. By doing this, the penitent one is saying that he wishes to be counted as innocent as an unborn child. This identification with the innocence of a child in the womb also emphasizes that there remains no more personally committed sin.

The principle of identifying with innocence is a thread that runs through many religious rituals in Africa and around the world.

One thing that strikes me is the willingness of the offended villagers to accept this ritual as sufficient and to receive the offender into full fellowship.

The Africans in Uganda place more power in a broken egg ritual than most Christians place in the blood of Christ.

I know mature Christians who are still carrying grudges over things that happened ten or even fifty years ago.

Is there someone you refuse to forgive and accept? Even in spite of Christ's blood? For shame!

Ephesians 4:32 says, "And be ye kind one to another, tenderhearted, forgiving one another, even as God for Christ's sake hath forgiven you."

Do the words "even as" leap off the page and into your heart? They should, for this clearly means that as God did for us, so we are to forgive others on the basis of the finished work of Christ and *not* on any human merit. The forgiveness of Christ is the *outrageous* kind that we are to freely give in His name.

Day 26

Flabbergasting Forgiveness

When we're young we do some stupid things.

—Gloria Richardson

An article in the Wednesday, August 7, 2007, *Atlanta Journal-Constitution* is worthy of comment simply because it is in the news. The fact that it is newsworthy is a sad commentary on the true state of Christianity in our nation, especially in such a widely churched city as Atlanta, which boasts a plethora of mega-churches.

After a concert by Korn on the fateful night of July 30, 2006, twenty-five-year-old Michael Scott Axley threw a punch, knocking down thirty-year-old Andrew Richardson. Andrew hit his head on the curb and never regained consciousness. He died four days later.

So, who cares?

His mother for one.

Mrs. Gloria Richardson appeared in the Fulton County Court at the sentencing of Michael Axley, who had pleaded guilty to manslaughter, to ask the judge for leniency toward her son's killer. On the stand, Mrs. Richardson said, "When we're young, we do some stupid things; I believe this young man would do anything he could to undo what's happened. This young man, although he was brutal in his actions, did something he regrets deeply. He's realized the impact his mistakes had on other people."1.

The prosecutor, Chuck Boring, said, "It's unusual to see this level of forgiveness, especially because the nature of the offense was so senseless." 2.

Bold forgiveness?

Michael was sentenced to ten years in prison.

Mrs. Richardson said she will visit him while he is in prison and added, "It's not just my faith in Christ that allows me to forgive Michael; it's what Andrew would have done, too. If he saw how remorseful he was, he'd say, 'Ok, man, I can understand that.' I can just hear him saying that." 3.

I recall, long ago, a man who actually went home to get a rifle because a new family was sitting in his pew at church. Of course, our churches do not have assigned seats, but past practice sort of nullifies our belief about such things. Thankfully, his dear, Christian wife convinced him that rather than shooting the offender, they would just go to another church.

O, such love and forgiveness.

Such forgiveness as Mrs. Richardson's should be so commonplace that it would not warrant space in a major newspaper.

Tragically, however, it is so rare that even religious newspapers are flabbergasted, as they recount such demonstrations of biblical forgiveness.

I do not know if I would be able to grant this kind of forgiveness. But I know I must find the power to do so if I am ever faced with such a situation, because Romans 12:18–21 requires it of me:

If it be possible, as much as lieth in you, live peaceably with all men. Dearly beloved, avenge not yourselves, but rather give place unto wrath: for it is written, Vengeance is mine; I will repay, saith the Lord. Therefore if thine enemy hunger, feed him; if he thirst, give him drink: for in so doing thou shalt heap coals of fire on his head. Be not overcome of evil, but overcome evil with good.

Is there anyone whom you should get off of your hobbyhorse and forgive?

Today?

Day 27

Forgiveness from Wilma

We are so thrilled that a wrong was made right, and that Wilma holds no hatred for the one who caused her much harm. 1.

—The Montoyas, Missionaries to Brazil

Claudia Norwalt sent the wonderful story of Maria and Wilma to me. I doubt that you will find either lady listed in *Who's Who*, but one day beyond the river, both will be on display as trophies of God's amazing grace.

Marie and Wilma were sisters-in-law, living in Brazil. When Maria's husband was murdered, she used her money to frame Wilma for the murder.

Wilma served ten years in prison for the crime, and while in prison, Christ came into her life. She bloomed where she was planted.

Twenty years after her conviction and imprisonment, Wilma was notified that Maria, now suffering with terminal cancer, wanted to see her.

Wilma has been a faithful member of the church started by missionaries Jake and Nancy Montoya. Maria granted Wilma's request to bring her pastor and his wife with her for the visit, but stated that she was not interested in giving up her religion.

Maria confessed that her conscience was bothering her because of what she had done and, on this admission, *Wilma assured her that she had forgiven her long ago.*

On her deathbed, Maria listened, as Wilma shared the greatest story ever told. Through her tears, Maria received Christ as her savior.

The Montoyas stated, "We are so thrilled that a wrong was made right, and that Wilma holds no hatred for the one who caused her so much harm." 1.

This kind of forgiveness—the kind given by Christ and by Stephen, the first martyr—is rare, but it should be the norm. I believe one of the purposes of Christian writing, preaching, and living should be to reveal to us where we are in contrast to where we should be.

I share the following with no malice or condemnation to the mentioned grieving families but as a foil for the normal, human response versus the biblical one.

Shortly after receiving the note from Claudia, I watched with bated breath as the case unfolded of a truck driver who had fallen asleep while driving and hit a car, resulting in several young people being killed.

Tragedy of tragedies.

What a horrific event. I have followed this story carefully to see if anyone who suffered from this loss would seize the opportunity to take the high ground and forgive this man outright.

The parents of the children were upstanding Christians.

I waited in vain.

The prosecutor in the case requested the maximum penalty, and several family members expressed disappointment at the leniency of the sentence.

I wonder if, in spite of their grief, the parents did actually offer forgiveness and comfort to the man who expressed sincere remorse and the media failed to report it, or if another opportunity to shake up a watching world was swallowed up by the desire for retribution.

Eternity will tell the story.

I thank the Lord for people like Wilma who, as poor, first-generation Christians, have a better grasp of God's forgiveness in Christ than do those for whom Christ has been "in the family for generations."

If we who name Christ ever start practicing His teaching, we will change the world in a few weeks.

Matthew 6:14–15 tell us, "For if ye forgive men their trespasses, your heavenly Father will also forgive you: But if ye forgive not men their trespasses, neither will your Father forgive your trespasses."

Day 28

The Great Hurt Back

Someone asked me why I speak and write on the subject of forgiveness so much. I suppose if my writing and speaking ministry is unbalanced, it would be in this area. There are two reasons for this.

1. I am sinner who stands in awe of the Love of God toward me in Christ Jesus, and who is forgiven and joins the saints as a joint-heir of God with my elder Brother Jesus.

2. In forty-seven years of experiencing salvation, I am still amazed at the magnitude of God's forgiveness.

1. Through His example and His Word, God has commanded me to forgive all who trespass against me in the same completeness with which He has forgiven me. I have a lot of trouble truly forgiving those who have done me wrong.

Today's grist for rumination is one that seems to be totally absent from Christian practice. The idea of willingly giving up any right, including the right of retribution for wrongs committed against me, is fuel for the fire to any red-blooded, Constitution-loving American Christian. I personally have little to no inclination to give up any rights detailed in the Constitution. Yet, in order to be a true-blue, biblically forgiving Christian, I must of my own free will give up certain rights in obedience to the plain teaching of Jesus.

Most of us rarely, if ever, really give serious thought to the doctrine of foregoing vengeance. This is strange in that the doctrine is clearly taught in the New Testament.

One Sunday evening, a visitor to our church gave a testimony about the impact of our church sign, which has a new saying on each side every week or so. I was amazed when I heard this very dignified saint share with us, "After years of turmoil over a sin committed against me, the saying on the sign set me free."

She then opened her Bible to reveal what she had written in the margin, "Forgiving means giving up the right to hurt back."

Folks, it doesn't get any simpler than that. It doesn't get any tougher either.

The right to hurt back.

Give up this right?

I have talked to ministers of the glorious gospel of Christ who, while they preach this truth, cannot give up the right to hurt back. They still carry a grudge of some sin committed against them when they were children, or when some member left the church years ago and told lies or the painful truth about them, or, more often than not, a mixture of lies and truth.

An observable truth within practicing Christendom is the ability to forgive those who trespass against us from afar, such as some famous Christian who has been caught in some sin. Yet, the same people lack the ability to forgive someone close who sins against them, such as a wife, husband, child, or fellow church member.

If true Christian love were fully activated, we would be far more able to readily forgive those whom we love the most.

One of my favorite passages on forgiveness is Ephesians 4:30–32. Many read it and fail to grasp the truth that God is teaching us to give up the right to hurt back, as Christ did. Check and see for yourself.

Ephesians 4:30–32 says, "And grieve not the Holy Spirit of God, whereby ye are sealed unto the day of redemption. Let all bitterness, and wrath, and anger, and clamour, and evil speaking, be put away from you, with all malice: And be ye kind one to another, tenderhearted, forgiving one another, even as God for Christ's sake hath forgiven you."

The word "clamour" has an interesting meaning for our purposes here. It means the cry of one's passions in railing against another, while asserting your own rights. Can you make any applications using that definition? Bitterness, anger, wrath, clamour, and evil speaking are weapons used to hurt back. We are not to use the weapons of this world as specifically stated in 2 Corinthians 10:4: "For the weapons of our warfare are not carnal, but mighty through God to the pulling down of strong holds."

Lay them down. Now.

Day 29

Dig Two Graves or Forgive

As an older pastor, traveling speaker, and famous author (famous to Mom), I am often called on to give advice and in some cases to referee fights among saints.

Mediating between Jews and Hamas would be a cakewalk by comparison.

I have learned to ask a few questions prior to committing my time (which is precious), my expertise (most of which has been gained by severe scarring), and natural brilliance.

The answer to one of my questions reveals much about the true motivation of those seeking my help: Are you willing to act in a strict biblical manner if you lose?

That our courts are filled with Christian against Christian is mute testimony to the fact that very few Christians are willing to abide by biblical instruction when they are faced with losing.

When it becomes obvious that the biblical course of action will not be adhered to, I bow out in my role as mediator with some advice from an old Chinese philosopher. If men will not obey scripture, you might as well share the wisdom of a heathen with them. Confucius said, "When seeking revenge, be sure to dig two graves."

Revenge—getting even for real or perceived wrongs—is becoming the focus of too many Christians. The Internet is loaded with supposedly funny forms of revenge, such as Revenge Lady.com (please do not give this to the Great Blond). All travelers to Mexico are more than familiar with Montezuma's Revenge, and from the Internet, I learned of Fecalgrams. The desire for revenge may be the natural mother of invention.

Society at large laughs and jokes about revenge, but the Bible takes a far different tact, teaching that revenge or vengeance belongs to the Lord. And when we usurp this prerogative of God, we are playing God, and He will soon teach us that we are not equipped for such a role.

Keep in mind that the Holocaust was Hitler's revenge for real or imagined wrongs. He got his revenge at enormous cost to his enemy, but at what a horrible cost to his own people.

It would be well for every Christian contemplating revenge under any color of reason or law to look again at the timeworn story of Esther and Haman.

This is what sensible people call the boomerang effect or the Haman Principle. The harmful things we throw at others have a way of finding their way back to harm us. Haman hated the Jews and built a gallows on which they were to be hanged. In the course of events, however, he himself was hanged on his own gallows of revenge.

Author and poet Giovanni Guarini said, "Revenge never healed a wound."

Which do you want: solutions or revenge?

And by the way, you can't have both lasting solutions and revenge. If you are too dense to heed the word of God, as least listen to the wise ones among the other heathens.

Since you have read this far, I recognize that you are at least interested in what God has to say about dealing with the bitter desire for revenge. I hope you have decided by this point to develop the habit of forgiving others, as Jesus taught with a graphic illustration in Matthew 18:21–22: "Then came Peter to him, and said, Lord, how oft shall my brother sin against me, and I forgive him? Till seven times? Jesus saith unto him, I say not unto thee, until seven times: but, until seventy times seven."

Jesus taught that by doing something 490 times, you will form the habit of forgiving.

Keep in mind and heart the biblical instruction concerning forgiving others—not only enemies but especially friends and family.

He said so.

Day 30

A Debt Marked Paid

While reading an article on simple methods to take control of my finances, I saw a story that reminded me of a method that I have used for years to sustain the forgiveness I have given to others. This method has contributed to many nights of peaceful sleep, when the Sinister Reminder attempted to get me to relive the pain of betrayal, denial, or whatever.

The method is really a simple, old accounting procedure. When we used to pay a bill in the dinosaur age, we would write "Paid" on the receipt and record the manner and amount of the payment in a ledger, along with the date. The paid bill was then placed in a drawer (or a box) labeled with large letters, Paid.

Occasionally, a vendor or a banker would indicate that the bill was overdue. So, you simply went to the drawer, got your bill, and picked up the phone. The operator pleasantly said, "Number please," at which you stated two digits. The phone rang, you gave the person answering your name, why you were calling, and the date, manner of payment, and a receipt number. That was it.

I have a similar system for dealing with issues of forgiveness. Sanity demands that you do not allow a large pile of things as yet unforgiven to accumulate, because forgiving others is a command from God's word, particularly from Jesus. Obeying Jesus in spirit and action is reasonable. To fail in this area of Christian life results in the accumulation of much grief.

So, when Old Slew Foot, as the old-timers called him, digs up names, places, and events that have already been put to rest, I have learned to run to the Paid drawer, find the particular receipt, and note the debt and the price paid for the person involved to be forgiven—released from that debt. That price is always the precious blood of Jesus Christ, the most precious commodity in all of creation. This is the price without comparable value.

Once a bill has been paid, no further legitimate action can be taken.

This simple procedure casts aside the humanly unanswerable questions regarding the sincerity, remorse, or repentance of the debtor. Thus, the long, insanely complicated list of sins, thoughts, intentions and slights, ad infinitum, that many have is left in the hands of God. As for making me "whole," a common term in legal circles, I am made whole by the priceless blood of Christ, and in His wisdom, He settles up with everyone involved. He makes no mistakes, and I go to sleep.

This is a pretty good deal, particularly for me.

I am doing for others exactly what God has done for me. I am forgiving the person, not on the basis of their goodness, but based on the righteousness of Christ. Sounds a lot like Ephesians 4:32: "And be ye kind one to another, tenderhearted, forgiving one another, even as God for Christ's sake hath forgiven you."

To record my financial affairs, I use a little more sophisticated system, but it really does use the Due and Paid drawer method, only electronically. Sometimes, the Due file remains occupied a little longer than I like, because funds are low or nonexistent, though they are not put into the Paid file prior to the actual due date.

We all know a little about waiting for payday or the offering before bills can be transferred from Due to the Paid drawer.

There is no excuse for postponing payment of the debts due to be forgiven. This should be done instantly, since we know that there is only one currency for such payments: the blood of the Lord Jesus.

In the spiritual matter of forgiveness, by all means keep the Due drawer empty of things not yet forgiven. Seal them in an envelope and move them swiftly to the drawer marked Paid, fulfilling the words of the Lord in Hebrews 10:17: "And their sins and iniquities will I remember no more."

It is my sincere prayer that you will reread this book at least once each year, because these pages aggressively teach the highest level of Christlike forgiveness. The world has witnessed plenty of the lower levels.

One final example of the kind of outrageous forgiveness the world needs to see is recorded in the spring 2001 issue of *Leadership Magazine.*

A South African woman is speaking to a packed courtroom, "Mr. Van de Brock took all my family away from me, and I still have a lot of love to give. Twice a month, I would like for him to come to the ghetto and spend a day with me so I can be a mother to him. And I would like Mr. Van de Brock to know that he is forgiven by God, and that I forgive him too. I would like to embrace him so he can know my forgiveness is real."

Instantly, the courtroom witnesses broke into the song "Amazing Grace."

Those who act in grace know nothing of the Western, watered-down version of sins too enormous for outright forgiveness but rather just do what Jesus demonstrated.

This is enormous. Mr. Van de Brock, while a policeman under the old regime, had taken this dear lady's eighteen-year-old son, run a spit through him, and roasted him to ashes, scattering the ashes to destroy any evidence. Eight years later, Mr. Van de Brock returned and murdered the husband. The wife was forced to watch, as her husband was bound to a pile of wood, soaked with gasoline, and set on fire.

The wife's above response was in answer to the judge who asked, "What do you want from Mr. Van de Brock?"

The sister in this account did not get to hug Mr. Van de Brock right away, as he had fainted when she offered her sentence of grace. When we who name Jesus Christ as Lord of our life start practicing forgiveness as taught and demonstrated by Jesus, the world will, in all likelihood, faint.

I sincerely hope and pray that you will begin living the life of a forgiving person in the name of and for the glory of Christ.

Ephesians 4:32: "And be ye kind one to another, tenderhearted, forgiving one another, even as God for Christ's sake hath forgiven you."

AMEN.

Day One

1. Hope For Your Heart, Carol Hoikkala Editor PO Box 23351 Minneapolis, MN 55423

Day Four

1. Cecil Whig 601 N. Bridge Street Elkton, MD 21921 Article some time in 2004

2. Baltimore Sun, August 9, 2011 Peter Herman, Making the most of a 2nd Chance amazing follow up in Emily Wessel. http://articles.baltimoresun.com/2009-08-09/news/0908080044_1_hinkel-wessel-judge

Day Five

1. Lewis B. Smedes http://thinkexist.com/quotes/lewis_b._smedes/

Day Six

1. Wherever you go, there you are. Jon Kabat-Zinn Hyperion 1994. Hyperion 114 Fifth Avenue New York, NY 10011

2. Ibid

3. God's World and You. O A Battista Pubisher: Milwaukee, WI Bruce Pub. Co. 1957

Day Eight

1. Marlene Dietrich, Ungar, no address but also on Brainy Quotes.com

Day Nine

1. Bone to Pick: Of Reconciliation, Reparation, and Revenge. Washington Square Press, 1230 Avenue of The Americas, New York. NY 10020

2. Forgiveness is a Choice, Robert Enright, APA Lifetools, American Psychological Association 750 First Street ,NE Washington, D.C. 20002

Day Eleven

1. http://www.brainyquote.com/quotes/quotes/r/ralphwaldo108803.html

Day Twelve

1. Mere Christianity, C.S. Lewis, Touchstone Publishers, 1230 Avenue of the Americas New York, New York 10020

Day Fifteen

1. 911 Handbook Kent Crockett, Hendrickson Publishers INC, 140 Summit St, Peabody, MA, 01960-5156

2. Janis Christy, Outrageous Forgiveness in 30 Days, Editor/Advisor

Day Seventeen

1. You're a very lovely daughter http://www.cbsnews.com/stories/2003/12/17/60II/main589107.shtml?tag=contentMain;contentBody

Day Eighteen

1. Mark Twain http://www.quotegarden.com/forgiveness.html

Day Twenty

1. Charles Gibson, Amish Say They Forgive School Shooter Nickle Mines, PA Oct 3, 2006 ABC News http://abcnews.go.com/WNT/story?id=2523941&page=1

2. Amish Grace. How Forgiveness Transcended Tragedy, Donald Kraybill, Jossey-Bass, PO Box 20345 Hot Springs, AR 71903

3. http://thinkexist.com/quotes/paul_boese/

Day Twenty One

1. Carbine Williams 1952 Movie starring James Stewart. http://www.imdb.com/title/tt0044480/

2. MacArthur on rifle http://faceprint.com/~walpd/gen/moore/carbine_williams.htm

Day Twenty Five

1. Heard on radio broadcast on Interstate in rural New York. I have searched high and low for the exact quote. However a search via Internet on the subject of Unganda, Genocide and Forgiveness is well spent.

Day Twenty Six

1. Fulton County District Attorney http://www.atlantada.org/latestnews/pressreleases/080607.htm

2. Ibid

3. Ibid

Day Twenty Seven

1. Hank Montonya, Cauxa Postal 141, 78900 Porto Velho, Rondonia, Brazil

Day Twenty Nine

1. Confucius, The Quotations Page http://www.quotationspage.com/quotes/Confucius/

Day Thirty

1. Leadership Journal is published quarterly by Christianity Today International, 465 Gundersen Drive, Carol Stream, Illinois 60188.

About the Author

Larry was born in Havre de Grace, Maryland, September 13, 1941. He is the fifth of nine children. Larry was educated in the Cecil County school system to the consternation of many teachers. He did additional studies at Maryland Bible Institute, and has an honorary doctor of divinity degree from Faith Seminary. Larry is in his forty-seventh year of marriage to the former Joyce Gore. They have four children: Jeanne (Frank), Jennifer, Dawn, and Dr. Jonathan Lilly (Stephanie). Larry has pastored churches for forty-nine years, served in Kiwanis clubs, was president of Premier Toastmasters, and is a Paul Harris Fellow of Rotary International. Larry currently publishes a daily Internet letter; the monthly printed *Larry Lilly's Journal*, featuring help for prisoners; and also conducts extensive correspondence with women on death row. The prison ministry is an offshoot of Larry's own experience in federal prison.

Larry has been the pastor of Berean Baptist Church in Terre Haute, Indiana, since June of 1990.